Taking Back Your Credit!
The DIY Toolkit

A Simplified Guide to Fix Bad Credit

Brittney B. Kay

Brittney B. Kay

Copyright

Published by:
Kings Resource Group
Atlanta, GA
WWW.KingsResourceGroup.com

ISBN: 979-8-218-64922-7

First Edition: March 2025

Disclaimer

This book is intended for educational purposes only. It does not constitute legal, accounting, financial, or professional advice. Please consult a qualified financial or legal professional before making financial decisions. The author does not guarantee the accuracy or adequacy of the information presented. The user assumes all legal, emotional, and financial responsibility associated with applying the information in this book. It is strongly recommended that you verify all information before using it. This book represents the author's interpretation of publicly available information. The author is not affiliated with any government agencies, consumer reporting agencies, or other entities mentioned in this book.

For more information on credit rights and resources, visit www.ftc.gov, www.consumerfinance.gov, or the CFPB website.

Acknowledgements

First, I want to thank God for giving me the wisdom, words, and perseverance to complete this project. Throughout this journey, God has been my strength, offering clarity and motivation in moments of doubt. Next, I extend my deepest gratitude to my children, my aunt Carol, my close friends Jessica and Jamaal, and my brother, Chris. They have all been my biggest supporters. They have spoken life over my vision, held me accountable, and selflessly sacrificed alongside me, showing patience and grace as I navigated this process. Lastly, I want to thank you for picking up this book. It is no coincidence that you are here at this very moment.

Preface

We live in an era of information overload, and one can easily find themselves drowning in a sea of overly complicated data and processes that just aren't practical for everyday use. If you have ever experienced this feeling, you are not alone. My name is Brittney B. Kay, known to many as B. Kay, and I help people overcome challenges, achieve their goals, and improve their quality of life. I am a certified life coach specializing in the areas of personal development, financial literacy, and essential life skills for success. Over the years, I have had the privilege of working with and supporting many incredible people on their personal development journeys. And in doing so, I realized that for many, the challenge was not a lack of desire for improvement, but rather a lack of access to effective and practical resources, tools, and processes. This realization fueled my passion for simplifying complex processes and equipping people in an innovative and practical way. My desire to impact others and expand my reach outside of my immediate community led to the birthing of this book and many more to come.

Doing something different always comes with its challenges. Though the processes in this book are simple, I cannot guarantee that implementing these steps will be easy. However, I can guarantee that you will grow from it. If you do not want to grow and have all that life has to offer you, this may not be the book for you.

I too faced my own set of challenges with writing this book There were times when I felt overwhelmed, juggling family responsibilities, a demanding work schedule, and the sheer weight of transforming complex credit concepts into an accessible guide. Late nights, self-doubt, and moments of exhaustion tested my resolve. There were so many times I put the pen down and wanted to walk away for good. But God! The completion of this book is truly a testament to the power of perseverance. So, when I tell you that you can do it, I'm speaking from experience.

If you get off track know that it is okay to come back as many times as needed, pick up where you left off, and try again. Show yourself grace, affirm that you are worthy of the life you desire, and know that you already have everything you need to change your story. Even if you dedicate just five minutes a day, you're five minutes closer to achieving your goal. Change isn't easy, but you are the best person for the job. I believe in you and look forward to hearing your testimony!

Introduction To Credit

The Industry

When you hear the term credit bureau, it is not uncommon to feel slightly intimidated. Most times when we hear the word bureau, we think of a government entity. However, rest assured that the credit bureaus are not government entities. Now that we have that out the way, let's talk about what they are. A Consumer reporting agency (CRA) is a private business that profits by collecting and selling financial data.

The credit reporting market is currently valued at nearly $20 billion and is expected to reach $30 billion within the next eight years. It is a system that not only benefits the CRA's themselves, but lenders and creditors have also historically profited more from consumers with poor credit than those with good credit.

For example, consider the cost of a car loan as shown below:

Exhibit A: Interest Rates

$30,000 Loan 36 Months

		$8,504
	$5,871	
$2,856		
6 % INTEREST (GOOD CREDIT)	12% INTEREST (AVERAGE CREDIT)	17% INTERST (POOR CREDIT)

▪ $30,000 Loan 36 Months

9

For the same car, with the same loan amount, using different interest rates- someone with poor credit will pay almost three times the interest of a person with good credit. It literally costs you to have bad credit, and in return, creditors pocket more money.

The credit industry thrives on these disparities. Because of this, even when confronted with mistakes, many CRA's lack the incentive to correct errors in consumers' credit reports because it subtracts from their bottom line. They literally bank on everyday people like you and I, not catching the errors and not knowing our rights.

The credit repair industry is expected to continue growing at a rapid rate. And as long as there are entities that profit from bad credit, there will be others who profit from repairing credit. While some professionals offer genuine help, many self-proclaimed "credit gurus" and companies promise quick results and miracle fixes that rarely deliver long-term results. If you choose to pay for a credit repair service, please do your due diligence when vetting the person or company.

Interactive Check-In:

1. What is a Consumer Reporting Agency (CRA)?
A. A private company that collects and sells consumer financial data.

2. Why do lenders benefit more from consumers with bad credit?
A. Because they can charge higher interest rates, leading to increased profits.

3. What should you do before hiring a credit repair service?
A. Research the company, read reviews, and look for red flags.

Your Rights

The U.S. government has established several laws to protect consumers from unfair credit practices. Understanding your rights allows you to dispute inaccuracies on your credit report and act against unfair practices. Some key legislation includes:

Equal Credit Opportunity Act (ECOA) – Prohibits credit discrimination based on race, gender, age, or other protected characteristics.

Fair Credit Reporting Act (FCRA) is a federal law created to regulate the collection and use of consumer credit information. It addresses fairness, accuracy, and privacy of information collected and used by the credit reporting agencies. There are several sections to this law, but overall, it states that all information reported on your credit report must be complete, verifiable, and up to date. (Targeted towards Credit reporting agencies: Equifax, TransUnion, Experian, any private companies that collect and sell information about a consumer's credit history and creditworthiness)

Fair Debt Collection Practices Act (FDCPA) is a federal law that controls debt collection practices. It prevents debt collection companies from using deceptive, unethical, or intimidating tactics to collect debts from consumers. This law generally outlines appropriate behavior of debt collectors when attempting to collect a debt. (Targeted towards debt collectors: collection agencies, attorneys, and any company that collects debt)

Consumer Financial Protection Bureau (CFPB) is an independent government agency that is responsible for protecting consumers in the financial sector and enforcing consumer laws. The CFPB promotes financial education and helps consumers navigate financial choices and act against predatory companies and practices. They enforce the FCRA laws (Targeted more on financial institutions; includes banks, credit unions, and other entities that offer consumer financial services/ products)

Federal Trade Commission (FTC) is an independent government agency that enforces federal consumer protection laws, federal competition, and antitrust laws. They regulate the Credit bureaus and share authority with the CFPB to enforce consumer laws. (Primarily enforces the Fair Credit Reporting Act (FCRA) which applies to all consumer reporting agencies includes financial products/ services by non-bank entities)

What is Credit?

Credit is an agreement that allows you to borrow money or receive services now and repay later under set terms. Your credit score—a three-digit number—reflects your creditworthiness, or the likelihood that you will repay debts responsibly. Your credit report, on the other hand, is a comprehensive record of your financial history, including debt obligations, credit activity, and account statuses.

How Your Credit is Used

In most cases you must give written / expressed permission for anyone to access your credit report. Your credit report gives others insight into your general trustworthiness, financial responsibility & can indicate risk of theft or fraud. A poor credit score can result in higher interest rates, larger security deposits, or even denial of services, & employment opportunities.

Lenders – Banks, credit unions, and other lenders review your credit report before approving loans, mortgages, or credit cards.

Landlords – Property managers and landlords use credit reports to evaluate rental applications.

Employers – Some employers check credit reports for positions that involve financial responsibilities.

Insurance Companies – Many insurers use credit scores to determine rates for auto and home insurance.

Utility and Service Providers – Some companies check your credit before setting up accounts for services like electricity, internet, and phone plans.

The good news is bad credit doesn't stay on your record forever. Negative marks will generally fall off your credit after 7 years, with a few exceptions. Bankruptcy – 10 years, Tax Liens – 7 years from the date you paid off the debt, U.S government & certain student loans – up to 7 years after action from the creditor is taken, Lawsuits – time varies case by case.

Obtaining Your Credit Report

A credit bureau or credit reporting agency is a company that collects credit data and sells credit reports or scores. The three primary credit bureaus in the U.S. are Equifax, Experian, and TransUnion. You are entitled to one free credit report per year from each of these agencies through AnnualCreditReport.com.

Additionally, various paid and free services offer credit monitoring and reporting. Research and select a service that best fits your needs.

Reading Your Credit Report

Most credit reports include four major sections:

Personal Information – Includes identifying details such as name, birthdate, social security number, and previous addresses.

Public Records – Lists financial judgments, bankruptcies, tax liens, and legal suits.

Credit Inquiries – Displays entities that have accessed your credit report within the past two years.

Accounts – Details active and closed accounts, including credit cards, loans, balances, and payment history.

Your Credit Score

All the information on your report is used to calculate your credit score. This calculation is done by a credit scoring model; a mathematic algorithm that predicts your likelihood of defaulting on your debt obligations based on various factors and the weight assigned to those factors. In the U.S. FICO scores are the most used. There are several different FICO scoring models in which the factors and weight used slightly differ. However, you don't have to get too deep into each specific models if you understand the commonly used scoring formula below:

35% Payment History – Making timely payments is the most crucial aspect of your score.

30% Credit Utilization – The amount of credit you are using compared to your total available credit.

15% Length of Credit History/ Age – A longer history generally leads to a higher score.

10% Credit Mix – Having a mix of credit types (credit cards, loans, etc.) can be beneficial.

10% New Credit / Inquiries – Applying for too many new accounts can lower your score temporarily.

Healthy Financial Habits

Changing your relationship with money is essential to changing your life. Wealth is truly a mindset. Here are a few tips for making that mindset shift:

Shift Your Mindset from Scarcity to Abundance
Recognize that opportunities to build wealth are abundant, and your potential is unlimited. Replace thoughts of limitation with visions of abundance, gratitude, and growth.

Practice Intentional Spending and Saving
Be deliberate with your money. Every dollar you save or spend should align with your personal values and long-term goals. Conscious spending leads to empowerment, not restriction.

Invest in Financial Knowledge and Self-Growth
Commit to continuous learning about personal finance, investing, and wealth creation. The more informed you become, the more confident and capable you'll feel about managing and multiplying your money.

Building and maintaining good credit requires consistent, responsible strategic action. If you fail to plan, you plan to fail. Budgeting is one of the easiest ways to plan for success in your finances. See the bonus section at the end of this book for my free budget planner.

 In this chapter, we'll explore key credit behaviors that contribute to a strong credit profile and long-term financial health.

Payment History (35% of Your Credit Score)

Your payment history accounts for about 35% of your credit score. This means that one late payment can significantly drop your credit score faster than any other factor.

Late payments include collections, charge-offs, repossessions, evictions, and other negative accounts. A payment is reported as late on your credit after it is at least 30 days overdue. You have up to 29 days after your due date to make a payment before it is reported to the credit bureaus.

Getting Back on Track After a Late Payment

If you've made a late payment, don't panic. You can take action to get back on track and minimize the damage:

Make the Payment ASAP – If you're within the 29-day window, pay it before it gets reported to the credit bureaus.

Call Your Creditor – If your payment has already been reported late, call your creditor and request a goodwill adjustment (removal of the late mark.) If you've had a good history with them, they may grant it.

Keep a Positive Payment Streak – A single late payment will hurt, but consistent on-time payments moving forward will help recover your score.

Consider a Hardship Plan – If you are struggling, ask your creditor about hardship programs.

Credit Utilization

Credit utilization is the percentage of your total used credit out of the total credit available to you. It is a factor that weighs about 30% of your total credit score and can greatly affect your score month to month. It is one of the easier areas to fix/change and see a quick increase to your score.

To get the utilization percentage for an individual account, divide your credit balance by the credit limit and multiple by 100 to get the percentage rate.

Best Practices:

Keep utilization below 30% – Ideally, aim for less than 10% to maximize your credit score benefits.

Request credit limit increases – A higher limit can improve your utilization ratio if your spending remains consistent.

Pay down balances early – Making multiple payments per billing cycle can lower your reported utilization.

Avoid maxing out credit cards – Even if you pay in full, high usage can temporarily impact your score.

Due Date vs. Reporting Date: Why It Matters

Many people assume that paying their credit card bill by the due date is enough. However, the reporting date (when the creditor reports your balance to the bureaus) plays a major role in your credit utilization.

Due Date – The date your minimum payment is due each month to avoid late fees and potential delinquency.

Reporting Date – The date your creditor reports your balance and activity to the credit bureaus. This can be before or after your due date.

Example of How This Affects Your Score:
- Your credit limit is $1,000. Your current balance of $900 is due on May 10th.
- You pay the full balance of $900 on May 10th.
- You make a purchase of $850 on May 13th. The purchase you made would not be due until the June cycle, so you plan to pay it down before its due.
- You were unaware of your reporting date, on the 15th of every month.
- You get an unexpected an alert that your credit score has dropped 40 points because your credit utilization is at 85%.

Though your due date is the 10th, your reporting date is not until the 15th, so any money spent in between those days will be reported as your balance, whether the balance is due yet or not.

Credit Age

Credit age is the average age of all your open credit accounts. It shows creditors how long you have been managing credit and is an indicator of your financial stability. It makes up about 15% of your total credit score.

A big misconception about credit age is that having an old account is the only factor. While maintaining older accounts is great, there are other factors that affect credit age, such as closing accounts and opening new ones. Managing your credit age requires weighing out calculated risks.

An example of these risks would be, opening a new type of account (which improves your credit mix – worth 10% of your score). Versus, adding a new credit card with a high limit (which improves your overall credit utilization – worth 30% of your score).

Best Practices:

- Keep old accounts open – Closing accounts reduces the length of your credit history and can impact your score.
- Be strategic about new accounts – Opening multiple new accounts at once can shorten your average credit age.
- Become an authorized user – If a trusted family member has a well-established account, being added can boost your credit history.

There is no one-size-fits-all approach to improving credit age. Please carefully review your credit report and financial needs to determine what is best for you.

Interactive Check-In:

1. What is the difference between the due date and the reporting date?
A. The due date is when payment is due; the reporting date is when the balance is reported to the bureaus.

2. Why is it important to know your credit card's reporting date?
A. Because high balances reported can increase utilization and lower your credit score.

3. What should you do if you miss a payment?
A. Pay it ASAP, call your creditor for a goodwill removal, and set up reminders for future payments.

4. How does closing a credit account affect your credit age?
A. It can lower the average age of your credit history, potentially reducing your score.

5. What percentage of your credit score is based on credit age?
A. 15% of your total credit score.

6. What should you consider before opening a new account?
A. Whether it will positively or negatively impact your credit mix and utilization rate.

Credit Mix

A diverse credit portfolio demonstrates your ability to manage different types of debt responsibly. A combination of revolving credit (credit cards) and installment loans (auto, mortgage, student loans) can improve your score.

There are generally three main types of credit:

Revolving Credit – A lender approves a set amount, and the borrower decides how much to use at a given time. The credit remains available as long as payments are made.

- Examples: Credit cards, personal lines of credit, home equity lines of credit. Affects credit utilization.

Installment Credit – A fixed loan amount with fixed payments. Borrowers receive a lump sum and repay over time.

- Examples: Student loans, personal loans, mortgage loans, car loans. Does not impact credit utilization but affects payment history and credit mix.

Open Credit – No set credit limit. Payments vary based on usage and are typically due in full each month.

- Examples: Utility bills, charge cards (with no preset limit), collections accounts. Affects payment history and credit mix.

Derogatory Accounts can be considered in the open category, closed category, or a general derogatory category of their own.

Types of derogatory accounts:

- Repossession – when a consumer defaults on a car loan and the lender takes the car back without (often without notice).
- Collection – when a consumer fails to satisfy a debt, and it is assigned to an agency that collects the debt on behalf of the original company.
- Charge off – a debt that a creditor has given up trying to collect and writes it off as a loss.
- Eviction – when a landlord sends your unpaid rent to collections or reports an unsatisfied real estate related debt on your credit report.

Interactive Check-In:

1. Which type of credit affects your utilization rate the most?
   A. Revolving credit.

2. What is an example of installment credit?
   A. Mortgage loans, car loans, or student loans.

3. What happens if you don't pay an open account?
   A. It can go to collections and negatively impact your credit score.

4. What is a charge-off?
   A. A debt that a creditor has given up on collecting and writes off as a loss.

5. What happens when a loan is repossessed?
   A. The lender takes back the asset (such as a car).

Credit Inquiries

A credit inquiry is a request to look at your credit file. There are 2 types of inquiries, hard and soft. A hard inquiry is when your credit is pulled because you apply for credit. A soft inquiry occurs when your credit is checked unrelated to a specific credit application and doesn't impact your credit score. Soft inquiries take place for things like preapprovals, background checks, or checking your own credit. Hard inquiries stay on your credit report for 2 years. Multiple inquiries within a short span of time could signify that you are having financial troubles or that there's possible high risk for defaulting debt obligations

Best Practices:

Limit unnecessary applications – Apply for credit only when needed to avoid excessive inquiries. Use rate shopping windows – For mortgages, auto loans, and student loans, multiple inquiries within a short period (typically 14-45 days) count as a single inquiry. Monitor your credit report – Keep track of inquiries and dispute unauthorized ones.

By following these healthy credit habits, you can maintain a strong financial foundation and improve your overall creditworthiness.

Interactive Check-In:

1. What is the difference between a hard and soft inquiry?
A. A hard inquiry is for credit applications and impacts your score, while a soft inquiry does not.

2. How long do hard inquiries stay on your credit report?
A. Two years.

3. Can checking your own credit lower your score?
A. No, because it is a soft inquiry.

Repairing Credit damage

FCRA & FDCPA Law Sections

- **605a (1-5)** – Period for credit reporting. The 7 years for accounts placed for collections or charge offs, 10 years for bankruptcy, civil suits. Judgments, and arrests 7 years or up to statute of limitations, paid tax liens 7 years from time paid.
- **611a(1)(A)** – right to an investigation: If a consumer notifies the CRA directly or indirectly of a dispute, the CRA is required to perform an investigation into the accuracy of that account within 30 days of receiving the dispute.
- **611b (2)** – Requirements for Reinsertion. If information that has been previously deleted from a consumer's credit file, is reinserted, the CRA must notify the consumer in writing within 5 days. (can use template for this specific violation)
- **623a(1)(A)** – Duty to provide accurate information. A person/ information furnisher should not provide any information to any credit reporting agencies if the person has knowledge or reasonable cause to believe that there is an error. (addresses the data furnisher of the information/ creditor)
- **623a (3)** – Duty to provide notice of dispute. If the completeness or accuracy of an account is disputed, the creditor may not furnish the info to any CRA without notice of dispute within 30 days.
- **FDCPA 807(8)** – Duty to provide notice of dispute. Communicating or threatening to communicate to any person credit information which is known, or which should be known to be false, including the failure to communicate that a disputed debt is disputed.

How the Dispute Process Works

You can dispute anything on your credit, but removal is not guaranteed. There are things that can greatly increase your odds, and in this book, we discuss them. Federal law requires CRAs to remove inaccurate, unverifiable, or incomplete information. But as with any business, not everyone plays by the rules, and the credit bureaus are no exception. Which is why you must be assertive and resilient in this journey.

You can dispute online, over the phone, or by mail. However, disputing online waives certain legal rights, so mailing a dispute is the *only* method I recommended. Mailing disputes is imperative for record-keeping and retaining your legal protections allowed under the law.

Once a CRA receives your dispute, they have 30 days to investigate and send you a response. Most disputes are processed using a system called e-OSCAR.

E-OSCAR

All disputes are automatically processed by a computer-based system called e-OSCAR (Electronic Online Solution for Complete and Accurate Reporting). E-OSCAR allows data furnishers to communicate with CRAs electronically. These communications use standard forms called Automated Consumer Dispute Verification forms (ACDVs) or Automated Universal Data Forms (AUDFs).

Step-by-Step Breakdown of the E-OSCAR Process

Consumer Submits a Dispute – The dispute is received by a CRA (Experian, Equifax, or TransUnion).

E-OSCAR automatically assigns Dispute Code – The dispute reason is assigned one of 26 available E-OSCAR codes and formatted onto an ACDV. It's important to note that over 90% of disputes are assigned the same 3 codes, resulting in an automatic verification. However, for anything that cannot be automatically read (more on that shortly) and assigned a code by E-OSCAR, a human ACDV clerk at the CRA is responsible for manually reviewing and selecting a dispute code; thus, increasing the chances of an actual investigation being done and your concerns being reviewed.

Next Request for Reinvestigation is Sent to Data Furnisher – The CRA electronically sends the ACDV through e-OSCAR to the original creditor or collection agency. The data Furnisher Reviews and Responds. The original creditor receives the dispute, and the 2 systems talk based on the data saved about the consumer.

The response is sent back via Metro 2. If the information cannot be verified, it is supposed to be removed. If the data furnisher's system "verifies" the account, it is updated or remains in the system.

The CRA updates the credit report accordingly. If verified, the account is labeled as "updated" or "verified." If it cannot be verified, it is deleted.

The consumer receives a final response with the results.

Metro 2 and Compliance Issues

E-OSCAR operates using Metro 2, Metro 2 is a format that provides the codes for reporting consumer data and guidelines for compliance with the requirements of the FCBA, FCRA, and EOCA, along with any state laws. It is also the language spoken between the data furnisher's system and the CRA's system.

Basically, when a data furnisher initially sends information over about a consumer to a CRA it is written in Metro 2 codes. Metro 2 compliance requires certain information be reported a certain way to ensure fairness and accuracy of the reporting process.

However, many times when data furnisher sends over their information, it is in the coding format, but not in compliance; meaning certain pertinent/ required information is missing, inaccurate, incomplete, or unverifiable. The system most times doesn't automatically pick up on when things are out of compliance. When you do a Metro 2 dispute, you are calling out the things in your report that are in violation of the Metro 2 compliance rules.

Many data furnishers fail to meet Metro 2 compliance, leading to incomplete, inaccurate, or unverifiable data. If a consumer disputes an account based on Metro 2 compliance issues, the CRA is required to ensure the data meets reporting standards. If it does not, the account must be corrected or deleted.

Interactive Check-In:

1. What system do credit bureaus use to process disputes?
A. E-OSCAR

2. What is Metro 2?
A. A standardized format used for reporting consumer data.

3. Why might an account be removed during the dispute process?
A. If it is inaccurate, unverifiable, or does not meet Metro 2 compliance standards.

Increasing Your Odds

Avoiding Automatic Rejection & Frivolous Claims

Now that you understand how the dispute process works, there are certain ways you need to navigate creating your dispute to avoid automatic rejection—better known as a frivolous claim—or other stall tactics that CRAs use to try to discourage you from pressing forward in the process.

Reasons Your Dispute Can Be Labeled as Frivolous:

Not providing enough information to investigate the disputed item.

The dispute is "substantially" the same as a dispute previously submitted by you or someone else on your behalf (i.e., using templates).

The data furnisher has already satisfied the applicable requirements according to the FCRA. (You resubmitted the same dispute without providing any new information or evidence to support).

In addition to your dispute being rejected as frivolous, you also want to avoid it being automatically processed as "verified" or "updated" when the goal is deletion.

Your Ideal Goal:

Have the item deleted automatically through system processing.

Get it into the hands of a human for manual processing/investigation, increasing the chance of deletion.

Some consumers use tactics like changing fonts, spelling errors, or colored ink in dispute letters to force human manual review rather than automatic processing through E-OSCAR.

Groundwork: Freezing Smaller Credit Reporting Agencies

There are several smaller CRAs that report information to the bigger CRAs. You want to freeze these small giants to increase your chances of getting items removed.

Why is this important? Sometimes when "verifying" information, the big CRAs rely on these smaller companies as data furnishers. Instead of conducting a real investigation, they simply match data in the system and claim it is accurate.

Our Goal: To force the CRAs to do their job by removing their ability to use these smaller companies as a shortcut. Here are some of the common companies you need to freeze:

- Innovis
- SageStream
- ARS
- LexisNexis
- CoreLogic

What NOT to Do When Disputing

- Never claim identity theft unless you are genuinely a victim of identity theft.
- Do not use templates or prewritten disputes (except in certain cases).
- Do not dispute online or through any apps.
- Do not apply for new credit while repairing your credit.

Dispute Types & Methods

The first thing you need to know is that there are two types of disputes defined under the FCRA:

Direct Disputes – Sent directly to the data furnisher or source of information.

Indirect Disputes – Sent to the CRAs, who then reach out to the data furnisher to notify them of the dispute. (You have more rights under the FCRA with an indirect dispute.)

There are several methods and variations of disputes that could fall under either or both categories. For the purposes of this book, I will focus on five primary methods.

Keynote:

Any dispute method can be used as a standalone or stacked with another method that fits your situation. I am not here to give my opinion on which methods you should or should not use. My only suggestion: Use factual disputes as the foundation—meaning that no matter what methods you use, the base of the dispute should always be factual.

Why? Using factual disputes as the base greatly reduces the chances of your dispute being rejected as frivolous. Keep this in mind as we dive into the five primary dispute methods.

Dispute Methods

Factual Disputes-Using facts (information on your credit profile or other documentation) to illustrate that something is inaccurate, unverifiable, or incomplete by showing contradictions, inconsistencies, or blatant missing information.

Your information across all CRAs should be reporting the same. If it is not, that's a sign that the information is either inaccurate, incomplete, or unverifiable. There are also certain things to look for that could indicate inaccuracies, incompleteness, or unverifiability, which will be covered shortly.

Metro 2 Compliance Disputes- Metro 2 is an industry-standard format for reporting consumer information that helps keep CRAs compliant with federal laws and regulations. The logic behind this dispute type is to call out Metro 2 compliance violations when information is not being reported correctly based on the standards that CRAs should follow.

Validation of Debt Disputes – When you send the creditor a written request to provide you with certain information about your debt (verification), as entitled to you by law under 15 U.S. Code 1692G FDCPA. Some commonly requested information includes:

- The name of the original creditor
- An itemization of the current amount owed, including fees, interest, and payments since a particular date
- The current amount of the debt when the notice was provided

FCRA Violation Dispute – This is when a consumer calls out specific FCRA violations, using specific verbiage and demanding deletion based on those violations. I won't dive too deep into this method, as it commonly involves using templates or copying legal jargon into a dispute.

E-OSCAR Disputes – The logic behind E-OSCAR dispute types is to make it very simple for the ACDV clerk or E-OSCAR system to know what code to select by using the exact verbiage found in the E-OSCAR coding when providing an explanation in your dispute.

Controversy Around Metro 2 Disputes:

Metro 2 is NOT federal law—it's only an industry-accepted standard for staying in compliance with federal laws. Because of this, it can be challenging to leverage or force the bureaus to comply with Metro 2. Some people claim they get great results with negative items being deleted using this method alone. Others heavily advocate against its use, claiming that:

- It is not very effective
- The risks outweigh the benefits
- It does not hold weight in court or formal complaints

Interactive Check-In:

1. What are the two types of disputes defined under the FCRA?
A. Direct Disputes (sent directly to the data furnisher) and Indirect Disputes (sent to the CRAs, who notify the data furnisher).

2. Why should you avoid using templates?
A. Using templates can cause your dispute to be rejected as frivolous because it may be substantially the same as a previously submitted dispute.

3. What is the purpose of freezing smaller CRAs?
A. Freezing smaller CRAs prevents big CRAs from using them to auto-verify data instead of conducting a real investigation.

4. Why should you use factual disputes as the foundation of all disputes?
A. Factual disputes reduce the risk of disputes being rejected as frivolous and provide a strong foundation for all dispute methods.

Reviewing Your Report for Errors

On average, 50% of credit reports have some type of error. However, many people do not know how to properly assess their reports for these errors. Do not fall into the belief that just because it is reported, it is correct.

All reported information must be accurate, complete, and verifiable. Something important to keep in mind – the burden of proof is on the data furnisher/credit reporting agency. If you have doubts about the accuracy of reported information, it's on them to prove it is correct, not on you to prove that it is wrong or to provide them with the correct information. Never tell them what the information should be. You only want to call out the general issue itself (e.g., inaccurate balance, unknown account, incorrect late payment date, etc.). Make them investigate and verify their records per law.

Make a habit of going over your report with a fine-tooth comb. Print or save your credit report to a computer so you can physically highlight any errors you see. Start at the top of your report and work your way through each of the major sections.

Common Errors to Check for:

Personal Information:

Check your name – it should be written out completely and spelled correctly. Even a slight variance needs to be highlighted as an error.

Check your birthday - it should be written out with the month, date, and year. Any variations (just the year, just the month, or any incomplete date) should be highlighted as an error.

Check previous employers and addresses

41

Missing / incomplete Information:

For each debt listed, your report must provide you with:

- The creditor's name
- The account open date
- The amount of highest credit
- The current account status
- The required payment amount (when applicable)
- The balance
- The payment history

If any of this information is missing, highlight it as an error because the information is not complete.

Inconsistent Information:

Information should be the same across all bureaus for each account. Check each account and go through line by line, comparing what each bureau reports. Highlight any inconsistencies and label them as inaccuracies.

Contradicting Information:

Information should make logical sense. Just because it is reported doesn't mean it is correct! Take an "if this, then that" approach when looking for these errors.

General Information:

Even if there's no variance, contradicting, or missing information, don't assume there isn't an error. Question anything you're unsure about.

Taking Back Your Credit! The DIY Tool Kit

Examples / Commonly overlooked errors

- **Contradicting Information (Charge-Offs & Collections)**

If an account has been charged off or sold to collections, then there should not be a balance due reported by the original creditor. You cannot legally owe a balance from the same account to two different people.

You owed a balance of $200 to Company A, who charged off your account and sold it to Collection Company B. Collection Company B now reports it as a collection with a balance of $200. However, Company A continues to report a balance of $200 on the account as well.

Error: Company A no longer owns the account. They can continue to report it as a charge-off, but they can no longer report a balance— that balance is now owned & reported by Company B.

Because recognize the account with Company A, it may be tempting to bypass the account and trust that it's correct. This is a common misstep that can affect your debt ratio by misrepresenting the balance for a total of $400, when the true amount is only $200

- **Contradicting Information (Monthly Payments on closed accounts)**

If an account is closed, then it is no longer open. If an account is no longer open, then it cannot have a valid monthly payment. Only open accounts can have active monthly payments.

Error: Many credit reports continue to report monthly payments on closed accounts, which is incorrect and affects your debt-to-income ratio.

- **Inconsistent Information (General information)**

If your account opening date is reported as 10/1/99 on Equifax, but shows 10/7/99 on TransUnion, that is an error. It is impossible for both dates to be correct.

Company "C" reports you owe a balance of $4,000, but you recall the balance being closer to $3,500. In addition, the high balance reported by Equifax shows $3,000 but Experian shows $4,000. Maybe you don't quite recall the exact balance, but there is no way both are correct. Highlight the balances as errors and make the CRA verify them.

Interactive Check-In:

1. Why should you never assume reported information is correct?
A. Because over 50% of reports contain errors, and reporting does not equal accuracy.

2. What is the burden of proof, and who does it fall on?
A. The burden of proof falls on the credit reporting agency/data furnisher, meaning it is their responsibility to prove accuracy.

3. What should you do if your personal information is incorrect?
A. Highlight any inconsistencies and dispute them as errors.

4. If an account is charged off and sold, should the original creditor report a balance?
A. No! The original creditor cannot report a balance once the debt is sold.

Your Dispute (Creating, Mailing, Tracking)

Now that you have done the groundwork and know how to comb through your report for errors, you will now learn how to compile your actual dispute.

In this book, we are going to focus primarily on factual disputes, which I consider to be foundational. To prevent disputes from being rejected as frivolous, the base of any dispute method should be a factual dispute. Feel free to stack other methods of disputes as you see fit. You will see some examples in the bonus section.

General Rules

- **Always include identification** – two valid forms such as a copy of your I.D., Social Security card. If your address on your I.D. does not match your mailing address be sure to include proof of residency with your current mailing address You want to verify your identity on each dispute letter to avoid delays and potential stall tactics from the bureaus.
- **Always do the groundwork**
- **Always mail certified** - keep your receipts with the tracking numbers, as well as save copies of each letter you send.
- **Set calendar reminders** - record the dates you send letters. Set reminders for when to follow up.
- **Check your report for changes** – regularly monitor your report, at a minimum 30 days after each dispute is sent.
- **Carefully check your mail/emails** - If you have an account with the bureaus, they may email you results. Sometimes, the bureaus send dispute results & correspondence in blank envelopes without a return address or other types of envelopes that can be easily overlooked or discarded

- **Be consistent** - follow up with sending each new round of disputes. Do not get discouraged if you don't get the results you wanted. The CRAs want to stall you or discourage you from advocating for yourself—do not give in!
- **Be mindful of any communication** – Conversations with creditors are often recorded and can be used against you.
- **Deletion does not remove legal liability** - Know that removing something from your credit does not eliminate the debt or the creditor's right to sue you in court. Creditors take consumers to court daily, it's truly the luck of the draw. If you are served to appear to court, contact a lawyer for legal advice. Do not ignore official court documents, it could result in a default judgement against you.
- **Always use your own words**—do not copy anything word for word, (except for certain templates in special circumstances).

Creating Your Dispute

You will create a separate dispute for each CRA. The format for each dispute will generally be the same. Do not forget to include copies of your identification.

- Date
- Header/Identifying Information: (always include your name, birthdate, social security number, and mailing address)
- Credit bureau/ company name to whom the letter concerns
- Each account number, company, Brief Description of the Problem/ error, & action to be taken
- Closing Information or applicable laws/ violations
- Any Proof, Screenshots, or Attachments

This doesn't have to be a drawn-out or complicated process. Once you have your errors highlighted, you will simply plug them into a letter using the above format. (You will see an example at the end of this chapter.)

Once your disputes are created, save a copy of each one for every bureau and store them for your records. Print the disputes, label your envelopes accordingly, and head to the post office.

Mailing Your Dispute

When you get to the post office, you want to completely fill out a certified receipt tag/form for each dispute you are mailing. When you mail them, you will receive a paper receipt for the transaction that has the tracking number for each dispute. You will also receive the bottom half of the certified tag you filled out, which also has the tracking number. KEEP BOTH for your records and put them in a safe place where you can access them later in the process if/when they are needed.

Tracking Your Dispute

If 30 days have passed and the CRA has not responded to your dispute, you can do the following: List your tracking number in your next dispute as a reference to your previous dispute, proving that they did receive it. Use this tracking information and receipt in formal complaints and escalations if needed down the line. Keep your paper trail—do not throw anything away!

Subsequent Rounds of Disputes

After Round 1, continue to follow the dispute sequence using the next applicable round. Each round should get increasingly more intense in the pressure you apply. Below is the general order you should follow:

Dispute Rounds with details

- **Round 1:**

Always dispute any personal information in the first round. You can do this separately or together with your first round of account disputes. I prefer to do mine together.

In this round, you want to state something that lets them know you noticed some mistakes and would like them to investigate.

List the account, provide a brief description of the problem, and include your call to action (delete, correct late payment, etc.).

Do not pull all your cards or stack too many methods or reasons in Round 1 in case you need new reasons later to counteract frivolous claims.

- **Round 2:**

Write something that lets them know you sent a previous letter (include the date of Letter 1). Remind them of the mistakes and why they were inaccurate.

Ask them to independently re-investigate and tell you exactly how these items were verified as accurate when you provided proof that contradicts their claims. List the account, provide a brief description of the problem, and include your call to action (delete, correct late payment, etc.).

- **Round 3:**

Advise them of each of your previous letters sent (include the dates of Letter 1 and Letter 2). Inform them that they continue to report inaccuracies despite you providing proof.

Ask them for:

- o Copies of documents for each of the accounts,
- o Who they spoke to from the original creditor
- o Details on how the investigation was done

Tell them you need them to prove that they verified and conducted an independent investigation according to the FCRA requirements. Inform them that it is not acceptable to just repeat what the creditor reported or go off an electronic response.

(Section 611 allows you to request the method of verification.) List the account, provide a brief description of the problem, and include your call to action (delete, correct late payment, etc.).

- **Round 4 / Filing a complaint:**

Before sending Round 4, file a dispute with the CFPB. In your dispute letter to the bureau, advise them of your previous letters and dates. Tell them that you are upset about the violation of your rights and have submitted a complaint with the CFPB. Provide them with the complaint number and tell them that you demand the changes be made as requested, due to the facts you have laid out.

List the accounts, provide a brief description of the problem, and include your call to action.

Interactive Check-In:

1. Why should you always send disputes via certified mail?
A. To track the dispute, prove the CRA received it, and use the tracking number as proof in formal complaints if needed.

2. What is the first thing you should dispute in Round 1?
A. Personal information, such as name, address, date of birth, and employer history.

3. What should you do if a CRA does not respond within 30 days?
A. Use your tracking number in your next dispute to prove they received it. You can also file a formal complaint if needed.

4. Why is it important to keep all tracking numbers and dispute records?
A. In case you need them for escalations, complaints, or legal action.

5. What is the purpose of Round 3 in the dispute process?
A. To force the CRA to prove how they verified the disputed item and push for deletion if they cannot provide the correct proof.

Alternatives to Disputes

There are a few alternatives to disputes that you can try before or after, however, I advise you to exhaust all dispute methods and rounds first. The most common method is pay for delete. You can mail a pay-for-delete request to the creditor.

Include the following information:

Account number, original creditor, alleged balance due. Tell the creditor that you are offering a one-time settlement offer for the alleged amount due, specifying how much you're willing to pay. State that the offer is not an acknowledgment of liability. Advise them that negotiations must be conducted with an official representative of the company who has the authority to approve such requests.

Let them know you are willing to settle the debt as a goodwill gesture under the following conditions:

- They must report to all credit bureaus that the debt is paid in full and remove any derogatory statuses.
- The payment will satisfy a paid-in-full status under the account.
- The debt will be deleted from their records.
- The debt cannot be sold, transferred, or discussed with a third party.

Provide your name, email, and phone number.

Post-Dispute Activity (No Reply, Verified, Updated, Removed)

After you send each dispute round, check your credit report within 30 days for updates. After Round 1, it is crucial to check all accounts under dispute for the "Notice of Dispute" comment (FCRA 623A). If the "Notice of Dispute" is missing- demand that the account be immediately deleted for failure to provide notice of dispute, which is a violation of FCRA 623A. (You can specifically call out this law violation in your dispute letter.)

For each item that comes back as "Removed" – your job is done! For items that come back as "Verified" or "Updated" – continue following the dispute rounds mentioned earlier.

Failure to Reply + Failure to Provide Notice of Dispute

If 30 days have passed and you receive no reply, you can substitute your Round 2 letter with a "Failure to Reply and Failure to Provide Notice of Dispute" letter. In this letter, include the following:

State that you previously sent a letter (provide the date) addressing errors you found.

Remind them of their legal obligations. FCRA 611 requires that they investigate disputed information within 30 days of receiving the dispute. If they fail to do so, they must delete the item from your credit file. FCRA 623A requires that they add a "Notice of Dispute" to accounts when the accuracy of information is disputed.

Inform them that 30 days have passed, and you have not received a response and/ or none of the accounts have been updated with the

Notice of Dispute. In doing so, they have violated multiple of your rights.

Request immediate removal of these accounts (or updates if applicable to late payments). List the accounts and include a call to action.

Escalations & Filing a Complaint

You are entitled to sue for damages for violations. Important Disclaimer: I am not a lawyer, so I will not go into detail on that. You can find more information about your rights to sue from the CFPB and FCRA websites.

Now that you have reached the escalation stage, my focus here is on filing a complaint. I will not provide a deep step-by-step breakdown, as there are several free online resources that offer better visual support. For a good starting point, search: CFPB Complaint Tutorial.

Brief Overview of How to File a Complaint with the CFPB

- Go to CFPB.GOV and click "Submit a Complaint."
- Create an account / Log in.
- Step 1: Choose a product or service for your complaint → Credit Reporting.
- Step 2: Select Type of Credit Reporting → Credit Reporting.
- What type of problem? → Incorrect info on your credit report.
- What describes your problem? → (Choose the most applicable option)
- Have you tried fixing the info with the company? → Yes.
- Did you request information from the company? → Yes.
- Follow the prompts and fill in the appropriate information until you reach the "Describe What Happened" section (Step 3).

- Writing Your Complaint:

In the complaint box, describe what happened and list the accounts.

Do NOT include account numbers or personal identifying information.

(See the Bonus Section for an exact template you can use, including laws.)

- "What Would Be a Fair Resolution to This Issue?"

Copy the list of accounts you included in the "What Happened" box and advise them of your call to action for each account.

- Attach Supporting Documents:
- Upload a PDF version of your latest dispute letter.
- Step 4: Enter the Company Name and your personal details.
- Do you want to complain about another company? → Yes, if multiple companies are involved.
- Step 5: Confirm your details.
- Who are you submitting the complaint for? → "Myself."
- Enter your address and fill out all required information.
- Final Steps:
- Review the complaint, authorize permissions, and submit.
- DO NOT EXIT YET! Stay on the page until all complaints show as processed.
- Track the complaint and stay updated on any changes.

Interactive Check-In:

1. What should you do before sending Round 4?
A. File a dispute with the CFPB and include your previous dispute details and complaint number.

2. What is a pay-for-delete request, and what should you include in it?
A. A pay-for-delete request is a settlement offer requesting that the creditor remove the debt from your credit report. It should include account number, creditor name, balance, and settlement terms.

3. What law requires a "Notice of Dispute" to be added to accounts under dispute?
A. FCRA 623A.

4. What should you do if a CRA fails to reply after 30 days?
A. Send a Failure to Reply + Failure to Provide Notice of Dispute letter demanding removal.

5. Why is it important to track your CFPB complaint after submission?
A. To ensure the complaint is processed and acted upon.

Bonus Items

Inquiry Dispute Letter

Paraphrase into your own words and be sure to include all header information.

While reviewing my most recent credit report, I saw some hard inquiries that I did not authorize. I have already reached out to the companies, and they confirmed that they did not have my information on file. Because I did not authorize these companies to pull nor view my credit report, these inquiries are fraudulent.

Please validate this information with these companies and provide me with copies of any documents related to these accounts bearing my signature. If you cannot provide documentation with my signature, I am formally requesting that the following unauthorized and unverifiable inquiries be immediately deleted from my credit file. List all the inquiries with the following information/ format.

1. unauthorized inquiry - Company name - Date of Inquiry

This investigation should be completed within 30 days. This is my final goodwill gesture to allow you to correct your erroneous reporting. I have been maintaining records of my communications to resolve this issue. Should you continue to violate my rights and operate outside of compliance of federal law, I will be using these documented communications to file a complaint with the CFPB and the Attorney's general office."

First name Last Name (DO NOT sign the letter)

Debt Validation Template

This is a template, and it is okay to send this letter verbatim if you choose. Send directly to the company that reported a derogatory item to the credit bureaus. Be sure to include all header information.

To Whom It May Concern:

This letter is about Account # Original creditor _, in which you allege that (I owe a balance of $__ / my account was charged off for $_). This is a formal notice that I am disputing your claim.

I am requesting validation, pursuant to the Fair Debt Collection Practices Act. Please note that I am requesting validation that is competent evidence, which includes but it not limited to the following:

• The original loan agreement or contract bearing my signature.
• Documents showing the alleged age of debt and date of delinquency.
• Itemization detailing interest, fees, payments, credits, and purchases.
• Copies of signed receipts for alleged purchases.
• Name, address, and contact information of the original creditor (if your company is not the original creditor)

Please be aware that any negative mark found on my credit from your company or any company that you represent, for an unverified or inaccurate debt is a violation of the Fair Debt Collection Practices Act; therefore, if you cannot validate the debt, you must immediately notify and request that all credit reporting agencies delete the entry. Failure to respond within 30 days of receipt of this certified letter may result in small claims legal action against your company at my local venue. In which I am entitled to seek a minimum of $5,000 in damages for:

1) Defamation, Violation of the Fair Debt Collection Practices Act (including but not limited to Section 807-8)

For the purposes of 15 USC 1692 et seq., this Notice has the same effect as a dispute to the validity of the alleged debt and a dispute to the validity of your claims. Please Note: This notice is an attempt to correct your records, and any information received from you will be collected as evidence should any further action be necessary. This is a request for information only, and is not a statement, election, or waiver of status.

Please send all correspondence to my address listed at the top of this letter.

First Name Last Name (DO NOT sign the letter)

Metro 2 codes

As mentioned earlier in the book, Metro 2 is an industry standard format for reporting consumer information that keeps CRA's compliant with federal laws and regulations. In this section, I will go over commonly required information under the Metro 2 Compliance, that you can use to point out errors in your credit report. I recommend reading this full section for understanding first, then going back to do your report.

Issue Identifier Key – Use the appropriate code that aligns with the specific issue at hand.

Issue Identifier Key	
Code	Definition
R	Required Information Missing
E	Error / Potential Inaccuracy
V	Variance / Inconsistent Info
Q	Questionable
M	Missing / Not Availble
I	Incomplete Info

Header record (HRCF) refers to the header for each account on your report. It should clearly identify the data furnisher, as well as the CRA that is reporting the file.

Header Record - Character Format (HRCF)		
Field #	Field Name	Required
12	Reporter Name	Y
13	Reporter Address	Y

The Base segment (BSCF) is the second part of a credit file. It contains consumers' identifying and account transaction information.

Base Segment - Character Format (BSCF)		
Field #	Explanation / Example	Required
7 / Account number	Account number	Y
8 / Portfolio Type	R (Revolving), O (Open)	Y
9 / Account Type	18, 37, 2a, 8a, og,	Y
10 / Date opened	Date Account Opened	Y
11 / credit limit	Assigned credit limit (if applicable)	When Applicable
12/ Highest Credit Limit	Highest amount of credit used by consumer/ original loan amount	Y
14 / Terms	Terms Frequency	Y
15 / Monthly Payment	Min amount due / 0 if an open account	When Applicable
17A / Account Status	11, 13, 62, 64, 71, 78, 80, 82, 83, 93, 97, DA. DF	Y
17B Payment Rating		Y
18 / Payment History	Payment history profile	Y
19 / Special comments	Any Special Comments	When Applicable
21 / Current Balance	Balance currently	Y
22 / Past due amount	Amount past due	When Applicable
25 / Date delinquency	Date of first delinquency	When Applicable
26 / Date Closed	Date account closed	When Applicable
27 / Date of Last Payment	Date last payment made	Y
30 / Surname	Last Name	Y
31 / First Name	First name	Y
34 / Social Security #	Full 9 digit social	Y
35 / DOB	Full 8 digit date of birth	Y
40 / Address Line 1	Street Address line 1	Y
41 / Address line 2	Line 2 of street address	When Applicable
42 /City	Full City name	Y
43 / State	Abbreviated State	Y
44 / Zip Code	Zip / postal Code	Y

How to use: Go through your report as detailed earlier in the book and find errors. You will outline your dispute as you normally would. Once you find errors use option 1 or 2 below to complete your disputes.

In your introductory statement to the bureaus be sure to mention that the accounts in question do not meet federal guidelines for reporting and that you are requesting they be corrected immediately.

Advise that according to what is outlined in both the FCRA and Metro 2 compliance standard you request proof for how accuracy and compliance of these accounts were verified. State that any claims or account found to be in violation, will need to be deleted immediately. (As always, paraphrase using your own words)

Option 1 physically mark your report labelling each issue with the HRCF # or BSCF # and issue Identifier (see the below at the beginning of this section). Please note, you will need to type out the key at the end of your report, so the person reviewing your report understands what the markups mean. Screenshot, cut, and paste each account with the markups into your dispute letter. Either above or under the screen shot, give a brief explanation of the issue and action to be taken.

Option 2 dispute without marked up report, using the dispute chart below. Create a chart like the following and list all errors. We see from the BSCF chart, Field number 10 is the date opened and it is a required field. In the below example, we are calling missing information from a required field (date opened).

Account Name	Account number	Metro 2 Field #	Field Descriptor	Issue	Violation Outcome
KTGH Bank	5555555555	BSCF 10	Date Opened	Date opened missing	Delete due to inaccuracy. FCRA 15 USC 1681e(B) requires CRA's to maintain accurate, verifiable, and complete info. Field # 10 required by Metro 2.

CFPB complaint template

In the "what happened" section of the CFPB it is okay to use pre-written responses/ templates, and or use laws verbatim. Below is a good template to use that gets great results:

I recently found several errors on my credit report and notified the consumer reporting agency. Even after making them aware of these inaccuracies & providing irrefutable proof, they continue to report these erroneous, unverifiable, and inaccurate accounts.

Under U.S Code 1681e (b) Whenever a consumer reporting agency prepares a consumer report, it shall follow reasonable procedures to assure the maximum possible accuracy of the information concerning the individual about whom the report relates.

Under 15 U.S Code 1681i (5) In general if after any reinvestigation under paragraph 1 of any information disputed by a consumer, an item of the information is found to be inaccurate or incomplete, or cannot be verified, the consumer reporting agency shall – (i) promptly delete that item of information from the file of the consumer, or modify that item of information, as appropriate based on the results of the reinvestigation and (ii) promptly notify the furnisher of that information that the information has been modified or deleted from the file of the consumer.

Please delete the following accounts immediately: List each account name, brief description of problem, and call to action. *Do not include the account number.

Affirmations for Abundance and Success

You've made it this far, so I know you're excited to welcome success and abundance into your life. Affirmations are the secret sauce—they help flip negative thoughts into empowering beliefs. It only takes about 21 days to build a new habit, so why not start now? Pick one affirmation each day to repeat out loud as often as possible through the day. Stick with it for a full 3 weeks straight and watch how quickly things in your life begin to shift. You've got this—your mindset is your greatest strength!

1. I am worthy of unlimited abundance, joy, and prosperity.
2. Money and success flow effortlessly into my life.
3. I attract wealth and opportunities naturally.
4. Abundance is my birthright, and I claim it fully.
5. I confidently pursue my goals and achieve amazing results.
6. I am intentional about my pursuit of knowledge and opportunities for growth.
7. I can overcome any obstacle on my path to success.
8. My mindset attracts financial freedom and endless opportunities.
9. I deserve the success that I am creating.
10. I release any unhealthy attachments and beliefs about myself that are not in alignment with the life I desire.
11. I am a magnet for wealth, happiness, and fulfillment.
12. My life is abundant in health, wealth, and love.
13. I am grateful for this new day and all the possibilities it holds.
14. I attract prosperous people and beneficial circumstances.
15. My income increases daily through multiple sources.
16. Everything I touch turns to success.
17. I am open to opportunities to selflessly give back and make a positive impact.
18. My thoughts and actions are intentionally aligned with the energy of abundance.
19. I celebrate the success and abundance that surrounds me.
20. I am the creator of my financial destiny.
21. I am living my dream life with ease, confidence, and abundance.

Monthly Budget Planner & Expense Tracker

Month: _____ Year: _____

Paycheck 1: $_____ Paycheck 2: $_____ Additional Income: $____ **Total:** $____

Expense Category	Due Date	Projected Amount ($)	Actual Amount ($)
Rent/Mortgage			
Utilities (Electricity)			
Utilities (Water/Gas)			
Internet/Cable			
Phone Bill			
Car Payment			
Car Insurance			
Health Insurance			
Life Insurance			
Student Loan			
Credit Card Payments			
Groceries			
Transportation/Gas			
Childcare/Education			
Savings/Investments			

Total Projected Expenses: $_____ Total Actual Expenses: $_____
Summary- Total Income: $_____ Total Actual Expenses $_____
Over/Under Budget: $____ *(Subtract your Total Expenses from your Total Income. A negative amount means you're over budget, a positive amount means you're under budget.)*

Notes & Financial Goals for Next Month

1. _____

2. _____

Discount coaching session.

You made it!! Thank you so much for reading this book through to the end! I am so proud of you for doing the work to Take back your credit! I hope you have found it helpful and will share it with others. I would love to hear from you and support you in your personal development journey. Whether it be to encourage you, hear your success story, or walk alongside you as your coach. My desire is to see you win in every area of life.

As a special gift to my first 50 readers, I am offering a complementary 15-minute coaching session. Focus areas to choose from include general personal development, goal setting, financial literacy, life skills, & business development. To redeem your session, visit WWW.KINGSRESOURCEGROUP.COM .Click "courses and coaching", and go through the prompts to make an appointment. At checkout use promo code "*Toolkit*". I look forward to hearing from you soon!